THE
TRANSFER OF LEARNING
POCKETBOOK

By Paul Donovan and John Townsend

Drawings by Phil Hailstone

"This is an important contribution to the practice of learning and development in organisations. By recognising the importance of an integrated organisation-wide approach to learning, the authors have developed a practical and powerful approach to delivering training that produces quantifiable results."

Kevin Hannigan, Head of Learning and Development, Matheson Ormsby Prentice

D1477810

Published by:
Management Pocketbooks Ltd
Laurel House, Station Approach, Alresford, Hants SO24 9JH, U.K.
Tel: +44 (0)1962 735573   Fax: +44 (0)1962 733637
Email: sales@pocketbook.co.uk
Website: www.pocketbook.co.uk

© Paul Donovan & John Townsend 2011

This edition published 2011
ISBN: 978 1 906610 32 6

E-book ISBN: 978 1 908284 09 9

British Library Cataloguing-in-Publication Data – A catalogue record for this book is available
from the British Library.

Design, typesetting and graphics by **efex ltd**.   Printed in U.K.

CONTENTS

4

WHAT IS TRANSFER OF LEARNING ALL ABOUT?

DEFINITION

Learning transfer is the application, back at work, of knowledge, skills and attitudes obtained in learning situations.

WHAT IS TRANSFER OF LEARNING ALL ABOUT?

COST

The importance of making sure that the learning acquired from training is used and not wasted is emphasised when we look at how much money is actually spent on training:

- In the US up to $200bn annually

- US employers invest around 2.2 % of payroll in training

- The Learning & Skills Council reported a £37bn UK training spend in 2008

- According to the OECD, the European Union spends 2.3 % of its total labour costs on training

Your country?	$/£/€		% of payroll
Your organisation?	$/£/€		% of payroll

HOW MUCH TRAINING IS WASTED?

Looking into research carried out all over the world, here are some of the findings:

- Training just doesn't contribute enough in terms of money earned versus money spent and skills acquired (Cromwell and Kolb, 2004; Barrett and O'Connell, 2001)

- There is a very poor transfer of learning back to the workplace (Broad and Newstrom, 1992, Facteau et al., 1995, Baldwin and Ford, 1988, Kaufman, 2002)

- When transfer **does** occur, only 40% transfers immediately, 25% after six months and 15% after one year (Wexley and Latham, 2007)

- One researcher (Goldstein) has suggested that 90% of all training is a waste of time and money – people either knew it already, forgot it quickly or simply didn't need it/ couldn't use it in their jobs

WHAT IS TRANSFER OF LEARNING ALL ABOUT?

HOW MUCH TRAINING IS NOT WASTED?

What's your experience of learning transfer?

Over a period of five years we asked training professionals participating in our train-the-trainer programmes the following question:

'What percentage of the learning that takes place on training courses for the employees in your organisation results in measurable performance improvement?'

The average stands at **24%** (ie respondents reckoned that 76% of training didn't get results).

What would be your 'guesstimate' for your organisation?

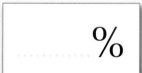

%

WHAT IS TRANSFER OF LEARNING ALL ABOUT?

KIRKPATRICK'S FOUR LEVELS

Of course, the 'classic' theory on how to evaluate whether training works is from Donald Kirkpatrick, who looks at the question on four levels. Basically, Kirkpatrick, who first presented his model in 1959, concludes:

- If they **liked it** (Level 1) they'll **learn something** (Level 2)
- If they learned something, they'll change their **behaviour** (Level 3)
- If they change their behaviour then the organisation's **results** (Level 4) will improve

Accordingly, Kirkpatrick was the first major author to deal with transfer, when he described his Level 3 as the application back at work of skills, knowledge and attitudes learned in a training situation.

Unfortunately, he was never explicit in describing just **how** this application was achieved.

WHAT IS TRANSFER OF LEARNING ALL ABOUT?

OTHER RESEARCH

Over the years since Kirkpatrick in 1959, many other researchers have delved into the factors which influence the transfer of learning.

Whereas Kirkpatrick's research has concentrated on identifying the outcomes of training listed in his four levels, subsequent research has attempted to identify the factors which help and hinder the achievement of these outcomes, such as:

- Learner motivation
- Manager support
- Training design
- Peer support
- Rewards

Building on these findings, this pocketbook brings to light new factors that affect the transfer of training back into the workplace.

WHAT IS TRANSFER OF LEARNING ALL ABOUT?

THE 17 FACTORS

We have identified 17 factors as the important things for the transfer of learning. These have been condensed from five years of research by Dr. Paul Donovan and from a combined 65 years of experience and observation from both Paul and co-author John Townsend. The factors have been soundly researched, and they make sense to practitioners. In fact it has been the HRD professionals' input that has been at the foundation of Paul's research.

- 28 senior HRD Managers generated 103 possible factors
- A questionnaire was developed and completed by 314 HRD professionals
- The factors were grouped/ shortlisted using sophisticated statistical techniques and then compared to other relevant research results

What makes the research powerful, innovative, and above all, immediately applicable is that:

- The top 17 factors were then selected according to **their impact on return on training investment** measured (using the Jack Phillips ROI model) after selected training courses were run in 11 different organisations

WHAT IS TRANSFER OF LEARNING ALL ABOUT?

HOW TO IMPROVE LEARNING TRANSFER

The research clearly shows that the amount of learning which is transferred back to the job doesn't only depend on how good the training course was. It also depends on:

- The importance given to learning and development by the organisation and whether the right training need was identified for the right person in the right job

- How well the training course was designed to meet that need and how well the learners were prepared for the learning experience

- How well the trainer(s) understood the learners' needs and how best to help them learn

- To what extent the learner was supported while trying to use the learning back at work

WHAT IS TRANSFER OF LEARNING ALL ABOUT?

HOW TO IMPROVE LEARNING TRANSFER

The way to improve learning transfer is to understand the factors which affect transfer and to take specific, facilitating actions at each stage of the training process.

STAGE 1	STAGE 2	STAGE 3	STAGE 4	STAGE 5
The Need	Design & Development of Training	Initiation	The Delivery	The Return to Work

THE TRAINING PROCESS

In particular, the importance of properly preparing learners for training is often overlooked – which is why we've emphasised it by making **INITIATION** a separate stage in the process model.

HOW TO IMPROVE LEARNING TRANSFER

BRUSHING THE ICE

Facilitating the transfer of learning can be likened to brushing the ice in the sport of curling.

The objective of curling is to slide a heavy 'stone' along the ice so that it comes to rest as close as possible to the inner circle of a target.

In order to help the stone on its way to the target, players with brushes smooth the ice in front of it – just as we learning and development professionals should be smoothing the way for learning to land on target!

TRANSFER OF E-LEARNING

This book is based on research into training interventions that incorporated blended learning techniques. Accordingly, the findings and recommendations outlined here can be used with confidence following this type of learning event.

The transfer of learning from interventions which are entirely digital in nature may involve a different set of factors – although at this point we suspect not!

Those readers who use purely digital learning technologies may want to test this hypothesis as they consider the impact of our 17 factors.

THE FACTORS AFFECTING LEARNING TRANSFER

INTRODUCTION

In this chapter you'll find an explanation of each of the **17 factors** that have emerged from the research, and from the experience of hundreds of HRD professionals, as being those that have most impact on learning transfer.

These are the things which can determine whether or not the skills and knowledge people learn during training subsequently get used to improve job performance.

By concentrating your efforts on what to do in each of these areas you can vastly increase your organisation's return on training investment. The section on Action Tips gives you plenty of suggestions to pursue.

THE FACTORS AFFECTING LEARNING TRANSFER

THE 17 FACTORS

1. Organisational support for learning
2. Organisational linkage of training
3. Quality focus of the organisation
4. Learner's organisational level
5. Learner's job design
6. Learner's motivation to attend training
7. Clarity of learner's job
8. Learner's job autonomy
9. Perceived relevance of training
10. Training linked to learner's job purpose
11. Career utility of training
12. Trainer effectiveness
13. Trainer's understanding of context
14. Training event climate
15. Learning transfer management
16. Peer support for training
17. Opportunities to use the learning

THE FACTORS AFFECTING LEARNING TRANSFER

1. ORGANISATIONAL SUPPORT FOR LEARNING

Plants and flowers can't grow unless the soil is fertile and people can't grow if their organisation doesn't provide the right conditions for their development.

Organisational support for learning was highlighted by HRD professionals and endorsed by the research results as having a strong influence on the transfer of learning.

Participants feel motivated and empowered to apply course-learnt skills and knowledge when they believe that their organisation values continuous learning and supports their own development.

2. ORGANISATIONAL LINKAGE OF TRAINING

Just about all the research ever done concerning motivation at work has shown that people will work harder when they know **why** they are working.

From the famous Hawthorne experiments at Western Electric to John Kotter's more recent studies, we have learned that 'effort is related to meaning'.

Returning course participants will give the effort required to applying new learning when they believe that the training was driven by important changes in their organisation and that their new skills will be useful in helping the organisation solve its problems and achieve its objectives.

Very Important Job

3. QUALITY FOCUS OF THE ORGANISATION

This factor refers to the degree to which there is a commitment to excellence in the organisation.

This is where you **don't** hear people say, when discussing their work results:

'That's close enough for government work.'…or…*'It's not perfect, but it'll do.'*

A quality focus exists in an organisation where there is an expectation that workers will always infuse the maximum amount of quality into their product or service. In order to do this they must be aware of where their own job efforts fit into the overall quality mission of the organisation.

THE FACTORS AFFECTING LEARNING TRANSFER

4. LEARNER'S ORGANISATIONAL LEVEL

Findings from the research show that those who perceive themselves to be more senior in the organisation transfer more to the bottom line than those who see their role as being more 'front line'. We have seen from this research that perception of seniority and control is quite a relative issue.

Many organisations work hard to invert the organisational chart where the customers appear on top, with those who serve them close by. As training professionals, it's our job to emphasise to front line staff their importance in the wider scheme of things. It's an old and true idea that if people feel important and powerful then that is how they will behave.

THE FACTORS AFFECTING LEARNING TRANSFER

5. LEARNER'S JOB DESIGN

Enriched jobs motivate people to produce better work and to transfer what they learn during training back to the job. In terms of job design, workers who perceive their jobs as requiring an array of skills, rather than just one or two, actually transfer more back to the job. This means that staff members must be helped to see the level of skills they bring to the table. It's no good assuming that they will know.

Every job requires skills. Even some of the most 'menial' jobs require a combination of motor skills and attitudinal skills to be successful. This is a task for the supervisor or manager. Are your managers good enough to help their staff to understand just how skilled they are? If they can manage this they will assist the motivation of their people – and the transfer of learning!

As Jimmy Buffett sings in 'It's my Job', a song about a cheerful street sweeper…

> *"…It's my job to be cleaning up this mess*
> *And that's enough reason to go for me*
> *It's my job to be better than the rest*
> *And that makes the day for me"*

Songwriter Lyman Corbitt ('Mac' McAnally Jr.)

6. LEARNER'S MOTIVATION TO ATTEND TRAINING

You can lead trainees to the conference room or the computer screen but you can't make them drink in the knowledge!

We sometimes forget the power of motivation in the learning process…especially when we plan some 'wall-to-wall', compulsory training for the whole staff group.

Not only can you not force someone to learn against their will, but you'll also have a lot of difficulty getting them to practise something new if they don't want to. So, **all** the research (and common sense) is telling us that, if we want to improve learning transfer, we have to find ways of motivating our learners to want to learn and grow (see also page 20).

7. CLARITY OF LEARNER'S JOB

Organisations grow quickly, bosses change and move on, administration gets lax and people end up firefighting to the extent that it's not clear just exactly who is supposed to be doing what. That's life in today's fast-moving world. But it's also one of the reasons training messages don't always stick.

Learners returning to jobs where their responsibilities are not crystal clear tell us that they haven't been able to apply the new learning. Or is it that they haven't wanted to rock the boat?

Job clarity, therefore, has emerged as one of the key factors in the 'ice brushing' process of facilitating learning transfer.

8. LEARNER'S JOB AUTONOMY

> *'After that course I really wanted
> to try doing things differently but I kept
> getting my knuckles rapped.'*

We've all heard this kind of frustrated lament from participants who feel they don't have the structural freedom in their jobs to put new learning into practice, and yet we keep tempting them with newer and more exciting training messages.

In some organisations it can be even worse – the bosses themselves block the practice of new skills either because they simply won't take the time to invest in coaching the learner or because they are literally jealous of the learner usurping their own position of power. Or is it because they find change threatening?

For learning to be transferred effectively, therefore, learners must have the amount of job autonomy needed for the effective use of new skills and knowledge.

9. PERCEIVED RELEVANCE OF TRAINING

Perceived relevance is just what it says on the tin!

Training which a learner sees, feels and hears as being **useful** to help them do their job better is more likely to be **used** to do the job better – whatever anybody else says or does.

The personally motivating aspect of this perception factor, when measured by performance back at work, is what got it onto the shortlist. If, at the same time, the training also helps the organisation meet its objectives then we have ourselves a win-win situation.

10. TRAINING LINKED TO LEARNER'S JOB PURPOSE

This factor has been shortlisted by HRD professionals and highlighted as one of the most important by the course return on investment studies.

Common sense also tells us that training that does not link directly with an employee's job purpose (however enjoyable) is unlikely to result directly in measurable performance improvement.

In today's cost-cutting, resource-sparse environments, training that is not essential to helping someone to improve **tangibly** their job performance has got to be questioned. It can be argued that happy employees are productive employees and that non job-specific training is therefore justified. If you think you *can* measure happiness and productivity before and after the training in pounds, euros or dollars, then we suggest you do take your 'feel good' training proposal to top management. If you think you *can't*, are you willing to accept little or no learning transfer?

THE FACTORS AFFECTING LEARNING TRANSFER

11. CAREER UTILITY OF TRAINING

Many a training manager is officially called Learning & **Development** Manager and it's the development part of the job that makes this factor so important.

It's obviously vital to use training to improve people's present performance by plugging gaps and honing skills, but it's just as important to help them develop new skills for future job challenges or for promotion.

Learners who feel that training provides an extra qualification for their CV or who believe it will lead to further learning and advancement are those most likely to apply what they have learned.

THE FACTORS AFFECTING LEARNING TRANSFER

12. TRAINER EFFECTIVENESS

Most trainers are justifiably proud of the role they play in helping people learn and improve themselves. However, a trainer rarely manages to do this by being a subject matter expert alone. Our research shows that, although competence in the course subject matter is important to the transfer of learning, even more important is a trainer's ability **to create the right conditions** for real learning. Those trainers who most help learners to 'take away' useful learning are those who are good at:

- Clarifying course content in relation to each participant's job purpose – during the course but even before the course starts
- Relating expected outcomes of the training to organisational needs
- Putting participants at ease right from the start of a training course
- Encouraging participants to share their experience with each other
- Showing commitment to the objectives of the training

THE FACTORS AFFECTING LEARNING TRANSFER

13. TRAINER'S UNDERSTANDING OF CONTEXT

HRD professionals separated this factor out from 'trainer effectiveness' because it's an important add-on to the skills usually expected from a trainer.

Understanding of context can't be taught on a train the trainer course!

Factor 9 is 'Perceived Relevance of Training' which refers to the content of the course. This is its human equivalent. In other words, the trainer (the 'messenger' who delivers the relevant content) needs to understand, literally, where the learners are coming from. What problems and issues do they face in their jobs on a day to day basis? What are their working conditions like? Why and how have they been selected to attend this training?

Understanding the context of the learners' need for training will enable a trainer to smooth the way for them to apply the learning back at work. The trainer is, therefore, a key member of the 'ice-brushing' team!

14. TRAINING EVENT CLIMATE

With 65 or so years of training experience between us we, the authors, are certain that good course design and delivery are essential to learning and transfer. Yet we sometimes forget that seamless design and smooth delivery may be taken for granted, or even go unnoticed, by learners – just as they expect a TV news team to select the most important headline items and report them in a professional manner.

What learners do notice, however, is that they learn as much from other participants on courses as they do from the trainer!

In fact, training event climate is the only design-related factor to have made it through the rigorous shortlisting process of the research. Humbling as this finding may at first seem to training designers, common sense tells us that busy course participants will favour learning that can be applied immediately to solve job-related problems. This kind of learning is what they get from picking other people's brains and sharing their own work solutions in a safe and friendly environment.

15. LEARNING TRANSFER MANAGEMENT

We could define Learning Transfer Management as the process by which a learner's manager smooths the way so that new learning can be converted into performance improvement – the 'ice brushing' that helps the new knowledge and skills 'stone' reach the target. Our experience has been that the lack of such a process in an organisation is the number one killer of learning transfer.

What the research shows is that transfer happens when managers prepare learners for training and then follow up after training by providing time, space and resources to enable them to put their new learning into practice. Without this infrastructure, there's a good chance that all the time and money spent on training simply goes down the drain.

There are many components to a good learning transfer management system and we hope to have covered most of them in the actions tips you'll find later in this pocketbook.

THE FACTORS AFFECTING LEARNING TRANSFER

16. PEER SUPPORT FOR TRAINING

A learner's peer group (their fellow team members) can greatly help – or hinder – learning transfer.

In our many years of training experience we've come across instances where people have actually been punished for trying to put the things they learned on a course into practice on the job. In factory environments, the punishment has been in the form of accusations of 'rate-busting' (ie working faster or better than the informally agreed norm and thus harming group solidarity); in office environments, in the form of criticism for rocking the boat or being a *teacher's pet*.

These instances, we have found, are exceptions to the rule. The rule is ...neutrality.

Generally, peers neither support nor discourage the use of new learning. They simply get on with their own jobs and leave the learner alone. This in itself can often be a hindrance to transfer. Why bother to apply new learning when you're the only one trying to do things differently and getting no support?

16. PEER SUPPORT FOR TRAINING (Cont'd)

When peers support and encourage returning learners, the magic starts to work and transfer happens. The research clearly demonstrates that, when learners feel that the team will be there for them when they start (sometimes with a struggle) to try out new ideas and skills, their performance improves and the organisation can actually measure the return on its training investment.

THE FACTORS AFFECTING LEARNING TRANSFER

17. OPPORTUNITIES TO USE THE LEARNING

'Use it or lose it' is one of those easily trotted out clichés that often prove to be true – not least when it comes to learning transfer. This last factor made it through to the shortlist for practical and theoretical reasons. Learning theory has been telling us for years that new learning will shrivel and die if there is no opportunity for the learner to practise. The practical results from the research have also shown us that learners who were not given the chance to use what they learned did not transfer new skills back to their jobs.

It's as simple as that!

On the next page you'll see how all the factors we've just described affect the whole of the training process from The Need to The Return to Work. After that we concentrate on **action** – what to do to 'brush the ice' and improve learning transfer and performance!

THE FACTORS AFFECTING LEARNING TRANSFER

THE FACTOR 'CLOUD'

Any one of the 17 factors can affect any or all of the stages in the **Training Process**, like a cloud moving above and around the process, as in the diagram.

1. Organisational support for learning
2. Organisational linkage of training
3. Quality focus of the organisation
4. Learner's organisational level
5. Learner's job design
6. Learner's motivation to attend training
7. Clarity of learner's job
8. Learner's job autonomy
9. Perceived relevance of training
10. Training linked to learner's job purpose
11. Career utility of training
12. Trainer effectiveness
13. Trainer's understanding of context
14. Training event climate
15. Learning transfer management
16. Peer support for training
17. Opportunities to use the learning

STAGE 1	STAGE 2	STAGE 3	STAGE 4	STAGE 5
The Need	Design & Development of Training	Initiation	The Delivery	The Return to Work

TOP 10 TIPS

Executive Summary
Vital actions to be taken to improve
learning transfer

EXPLANATION

These Top 10 suggested actions to take in order to improve learning transfer in your organisation are, in effect, an executive summary of the stage-by-stage, detailed *Action Tips* which are specified in the following chapter.

They are all based on the impact which the 17 factors have on bringing learning back to the job. If you only had the time and/or resources to do 10 things, these would be the ones to choose.

We've listed them in chronological order following the Training Process Flowchart from page 14.

THE NEED

TOP 10 TIPS

1. Conduct a relevant, rigorous and robust training needs identification and communicate the results so that it is stunningly obvious to learners that the only training to be conducted in your organisation will be that which is vital for performance improvement.

2. Don't be tempted to provide training which is faddish, flavour-of-the-month or frivolous. In other words any training which, however appealing, is not related to measurable performance improvement.

TRAINING DESIGN & DEVELOPMENT

TOP 10 TIPS

3. Demand that all exercises and other course activities that give participants opportunities to practise their learned skills and knowledge simulate their work environment. In this way learners can use the learning back in the workplace to help improve job performance.

4. Design into all training programmes sufficient opportunities for learners to get together and share the best tips from their work experience. (Remember, participants often say that they learned as much from each other as they did from the trainer.)

42

INITIATION

TOP 10 TIPS

5. Insist that line managers conduct a **pre-course briefing** with all learners during which they plan ways to link the training to **post-course** job improvement.

6. Prepare joining instructions which are motivational and which convey the essence, the purpose and the importance of the training.

TRAINING DELIVERY

TOP
10
TIPS

7. Enthusiastically welcome participants to training courses in a way that relaxes them and sets the stage for a warm and trusting learning experience.

   (This may sound corny but one of the key findings from the research into learning transfer is that participants who feel confident and who trust those around them are more motivated to contribute their best ideas. Similarly, those who receive ideas in this kind of environment are more likely to use them back on the job.)

8. Refrain from dominating training sessions with prescriptive teaching before learners have had the opportunity to explore their own ideas and develop their own priorities.

TRAINING DELIVERY

THE RETURN TO WORK

TOP
10
TIPS

9. Make meetings mandatory! Insist that managers conduct **post-course briefings** with all participants, during which both will assess the learning gained from the training and make detailed plans for its transfer to the job.

10. Provide adequate time, space and resources for learners to effectively implement their new learning. Accept willingly the inevitable (temporary) dip in productivity as the learner practises new job behaviours.

ACTION TIPS

OVERVIEW

This chapter is a compendium of 70 action tips for improving the transfer of learning in your organisation. We've divided the tips into five groups – aligned to each stage of the training process – and selected the key factors which affect transfer at each of these stages. This is not an exhaustive selection. Use your own judgment and creativity to identify how any of the other factors might also impact each stage.

ACTION TIPS

STAGE 1: THE NEED
KEY FACTORS

There are three factors most relevant to this, the first stage of the training process.

STAGE 1	STAGE 2	STAGE 3	STAGE 4	STAGE 5
The Need	Design & Development of Training	Initiation	The Delivery	The Return to Work

1. Organisational support for learning
2. **Organisational linkage of training**
3. Quality focus of the organisation
4. Learner's organisational level
5. Learner's job design
6. Learner's motivation to attend training
7. Clarity of learner's job
8. Learner's job autonomy
9. **Perceived relevance of training**
10. **Training linked to learner's job purpose**
11. Career utility of training
12. Trainer effectiveness
13. Trainer's understanding of context
14. Training event climate
15. Learning transfer management
16. Peer support for training
17. Opportunities to use the learning

ACTION TIPS

STAGE 1: THE NEED

EXPLANATION

All the research and experience we've gathered shows that:

- Training is more likely to be transferred if the participants think that their organisation believes in training their staff and that what they have learned will, in some way, help to solve some of the organisation's problems and improve its performance

- Training will transfer well when participants can clearly see the relevance of what they are learning and how they can use it back at work

- People are more likely to use the skills and knowledge they learn when they believe that these are in line with the purpose of their job

ACTION TIPS

STAGE 1: THE NEED

ORGANISATIONAL LINKAGE OF TRAINING

 If it's not already the case, propose to include training and people development in the organisation's mission and values statement

(This is only a first step. Whether or not an organisation 'believes' in training depends on more than just a mission statement. Above all, it depends on the tangible results provided by the training function...read on!)

 Regularly take the opportunity to pose the **three key training need questions** to senior management:

- What are you trying to achieve/ avoid?
- What must people in the organisation do to help you get there?
- What must they learn in order to provide this help?

ACTION TIPS

STAGE 1: THE NEED

PERCEIVED RELEVANCE OF TRAINING

✓ Based on the answers to the three training need questions, help the organisation create/ implement a rigorous system for determining what training is needed for whom, in order to improve organisational performance

(A detailed example, the **INVESTIGATE** model outline, can be found in the *Training Needs Analysis Pocketbook*, also by Paul Donovan and John Townsend)

✓ Assist management in briefing all staff members on how the training needs identified and the resulting training actions are relevant to the goals of the organisation

(For example, during induction training/ on the company website/ at conferences, presentations, etc)

ACTION TIPS

STAGE 1: THE NEED

TRAINING LINKED TO LEARNER'S JOB PURPOSE

 Resist the temptation to implement training which:

- Rewards good past performance
- Is not related to on-the-job performance improvement
- Is 'feel good', 'away day' or re-motivational in nature
- Is faddish, flavour-of-the-month or copy-cat training (ie our competitors/someone we know did some of this kind of training – so should we)

NB Learning and development staff who are learning transfer-friendly jealously guard their reputation as serious organisational professionals – refusing to be associated with lightweight '*entertrainment*'.

ACTION TIPS

STAGE 1: THE NEED

SUMMARY

Conduct a methodical identification of training needs within your organisation, ensuring at every step that the needs are always linked to organisational performance improvement and individual job purpose.

Communicate the results of the analysis, and secure the commitment of targeted learners and their managers. For further help on this topic, see *Training Needs Analysis Pocketbook*.

ACTION TIPS

STAGE 2: THE DESIGN & DEVELOPMENT OF TRAINING

KEY FACTORS

Again, three factors are particularly relevant to the design and development stage.

1 Organisational support for learning
2 Organisational linkage of training
3 Quality focus of the organisation
4 Learner's organisational level
5 Learner's job design
6 Learner's motivation to attend training
7 Clarity of learner's job
8 Learner's job autonomy
9 Perceived relevance of training
10 Training linked to learner's job purpose
11 Career utility of training
12 Trainer effectiveness
13 Trainer's understanding of context
14 Training event climate
15 Learning transfer management
16 Peer support for training
17 Opportunities to use the learning

STAGE 1	STAGE 2	STAGE 3	STAGE 4	STAGE 5
The Need	Design & Development of Training	Initiation	The Delivery	The Return to Work

ACTION TIPS

STAGE 2: THE DESIGN & DEVELOPMENT OF TRAINING

EXPLANATION

These factors have been selected to prompt actions at this stage of the training process because:

- 'Off-the-shelf' training courses or branded, 'one-size-fits-all' products are less likely to provide transferable learning than courses designed with specific, home-grown issues in mind

- Courses with written learning outcomes relevant to participants' jobs have higher transfer scores than those without

- Fellow trainees also contribute to learning on training courses

- Course designs which allow time for 'show and tell' sessions favour learning transfer

Roll up for the amazing

one-size-fits-all training course

every Tuesday at 9.00 am

ACTION TIPS

STAGE 2: THE DESIGN & DEVELOPMENT OF TRAINING

PERCEIVED RELEVANCE OF TRAINING
TRAINING LINKED TO LEARNER'S JOB PURPOSE

 Ensure that the course title and content reflect specific job issues

 Design and develop course exercises and activities that simulate the actual job situation of the majority of the participants

(Sometimes, especially in public courses, this may be difficult. If this Action Tip cannot be achieved it doesn't mean that the course is bad – only that it may not be as transferable as it could be!)

 Tools, tips and especially handouts given on training programmes must be obviously transferable and usable for each participant's job

ACTION TIPS

STAGE 2: THE DESIGN & DEVELOPMENT OF TRAINING

TRAINING LINKED TO LEARNER'S JOB PURPOSE
TRAINING EVENT CLIMATE

☑ Always provide physical space at course venues to allow people to mix and share ideas

☑ In all training courses build in opportunities for planning the application of the learning to specific job situations

☑ Create exercises which allow for sharing of existing best practice

☑ Build 'case conferences' into all courses where participants provide their own problems/ issues for the group to work on

☑ Design into all courses 15 minute coffee/ tea breaks at least every 90 minutes. Allow at least one hour for lunch to allow for participant exchange, chatter and camaraderie

STAGE 2: THE DESIGN & DEVELOPMENT OF TRAINING

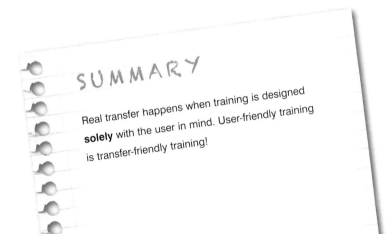

SUMMARY

Real transfer happens when training is designed **solely** with the user in mind. User-friendly training is transfer-friendly training!

ACTION TIPS

STAGE 3: INITIATION
KEY FACTORS

A bumper crop of seven factors now takes centre stage. It's all about being prepared!

1. Organisational support for learning
2. Organisational linkage of training
3. Quality focus of the organisation
4. Learner's organisational level
5. Learner's job design
6. **Learner's motivation to attend training**
7. **Clarity of learner's job**
8. **Learner's job autonomy**
9. Perceived relevance of training
10. Training linked to learner's job purpose
11. **Career utility of training**
12. Trainer effectiveness
13. Trainer's understanding of context
14. **Training event climate**
15. **Learning transfer management**
16. **Peer support for training**
17. Opportunities to use the learning

STAGE 1	STAGE 2	STAGE 3	STAGE 4	STAGE 5
The Need	Design & Development of Training	Initiation	The Delivery	The Return to Work

ACTION TIPS

STAGE 3: INITIATION
EXPLANATION

This is probably the most neglected phase of the training process. How often are participants on training courses actually briefed by their managers before they attend? On a recent one-week Master Trainer Programme, only two of the trainers participating had discussed specific expectations and objectives for the programme with their boss before leaving.

If trainers themselves aren't getting it right, then who...?!

The Action Tips for this stage suggest how managers can **motivate** their staff to attend job-relevant training by:

- **Clarifying** their responsibilities
- Allowing maximum possible **autonomy** in putting the learning into practice
- Demonstrating how the training can help them progress in their **career**
- Planning an 'ice-brushing' **system** of actions and/ or procedures (see pages 67-68) to facilitate the **transfer** of learning from training to job performance improvement

STAGE 3: INITIATION

LEARNER'S MOTIVATION TO ATTEND TRAINING

In the period of time leading up to a planned training event, participants' managers should explain the advantages of acquiring the new knowledge and skills in varied ways, depending on the learner's motivational profile and needs.

Examples:

 For an employee with a high need for **security**:
'This training will give you a 'redundancy-proof' edge over less qualified colleagues.'

 For a learner with high **social** needs:
'This training will help you integrate even better into the team/ be a resource person for the team.'

 For someone with a high need for **esteem**:
'These skills will increase your chances of job enrichment/ promotion and improve your visibility within the organisation.'

 For people who wish for personal **growth**:
'As well as helping the organisation meet its objectives, this training will help you to develop as a person and fulfil your potential.'

STAGE 3: INITIATION

CLARITY OF LEARNER'S JOB

Participants' managers must take advantage of forthcoming training to:

 Clarify learners' roles and responsibilities by reviewing job descriptions, job maps and other agreements as to who does what

A lot of training is wasted because learners are not clear what they are supposed to do with the learning back at work. It's even worse when bosses and/ or peers criticise them for trying out things the trainer has urged them to do, but that turn out to be outside their job description. If all this had been clear before they started the training, a lot of time and money could have been saved!

ACTION TIPS

STAGE 3: INITIATION
LEARNER'S JOB AUTONOMY

 Clarify the degree of freedom and authority the learner will have in applying the learning in their job. Not just **who** will be responsible for what, but also – **how far** the learner can go in using the new skills and knowledge before overstepping the mark

Most training courses encourage participants to take on new challenges, try things out, grow towards increased autonomy. Unless the boundaries are clearly fixed prior to the training, the results can be counter-productive – a potential candidate for expanded responsibility turning into a frustrated under-performer.

ACTION TIPS

STAGE 3: INITIATION

CAREER UTILITY OF TRAINING

The research results show clearly that achieving official qualifications and learning transfer go hand in hand, so:

 Training organisers must consider how to obtain accreditation opportunities for their learners. (In Europe, for example, the Bologna Agreement provides for a single European education and training market where qualifications are accepted on a continent-wide basis)

The research shows that participants who believe that a course will help them advance in their career will transfer more and thus contribute to their department's return on training investment, so:

 Managers must take every opportunity to show how training will help learners' careers. (At the latest, during pre-course briefings but also regularly at performance appraisals, project reviews, departmental meetings, etc)

STAGE 3: INITIATION

TRAINING EVENT CLIMATE

Groucho Marx once said that he wouldn't care to belong to any club that would have him as a member!

In order to motivate people to want to be members of our training events, we need to make the event attractive and demonstrate to prospective participants how important the training is to them and how important they are to the training. One way to do this is to:

 Prepare joining instructions and course outlines that are motivational and convey the essence, the purpose and the importance of the training. Design them to be professional and attractive

ACTION TIPS

STAGE 3: INITIATION

LEARNING TRANSFER MANAGEMENT (1)

Include in all managers' job descriptions the requirement to conduct **pre-course briefings**, during which they:

 Communicate clear expectations of the training and the learning. For example, prior to a facilitation skills course:

'I'm expecting you to learn enough about structuring and facilitating a discussion session to be able to take over the running of our department problem-solving meeting at the end of November.'

'I would like us to do an evaluation of the course content, delivery and relevance when you get back.'

ACTION TIPS

STAGE 3: INITIATION

LEARNING TRANSFER MANAGEMENT (2)

Include in all managers' job descriptions the requirement to conduct **pre-course briefings**, during which they:

☑ Coach participants in anticipation of the training. For example, prior to a leadership course: *'When the trainer explains the situational leadership model during the course, try to think of situations and styles which will suit your own team members.'*

☑ Brief participants on how the course should affect job performance. For example:
- Agree specific performance goals to be met as a result of the training
- Discuss how the learner will be helped to implement new skills on return to work
- Explain that temporary performance dips will be accepted while new skills are practised

ACTION TIPS

STAGE 3: INITIATION
PEER SUPPORT FOR TRAINING

How often are participants on training courses bothered by phone calls on issues 'only they' can deal with? And how large is the pile of problems left unattended to await their return? How much time and mental space does this leave them to start putting into practice what they've just learned? Many returning learners say this is the most frustrating part of going on a training course. To make it worse, they often hear colleagues, and even bosses, almost sneering, 'Hope you enjoyed the holiday... now back to work!'

As an antidote to this situation, which in itself counts for a large percentage of 'wasted' learning transfer:

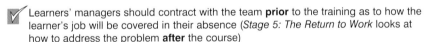

☑ Learners' managers should contract with the team **prior** to the training as to how the learner's job will be covered in their absence (*Stage 5: The Return to Work* looks at how to address the problem **after** the course)

☑ Whenever possible, managers could send a second 'learning buddy' participant to the same course. They can work together to ensure that their learning is really job-specific and, above all, prepare themselves to face the inevitable return to work frustrations by planning how to support one another

STAGE 3: INITIATION

SUMMARY

The learner's manager is central in preparing them for training – in clarifying the reasons for the training and its links to the learner's role, and in preparing the way for implementation of new skills when the learner returns to work.

ACTION TIPS

STAGE 4: THE DELIVERY

KEY FACTORS

The three particularly influential factors when it comes to the actual delivery stage are in the hands of the trainers.

1. Organisational support for learning
2. Organisational linkage of training
3. Quality focus of the organisation
4. Learner's organisational level
5. Learner's job design
6. Learner's motivation to attend training
7. Clarity of learner's job
8. Learner's job autonomy
9. Perceived relevance of training
10. Training linked to learner's job purpose
11. Career utility of training
12. **Trainer effectiveness**
13. **Trainer's understanding of context**
14. **Training event climate**
15. Learning transfer management
16. Peer support for training
17. Opportunities to use the learning

STAGE 1	STAGE 2	STAGE 3	STAGE 4	STAGE 5
The Need	Design & Development of Training	Initiation	The Delivery	The Return to Work

(71)

STAGE 4: THE DELIVERY

EXPLANATION

Have you ever heard that cliché, *'I learned as much from the other participants as I did from the trainer'*? Well, all the research into learning transfer seems to confirm this statement but, disappointingly perhaps, doesn't highlight any other area of training delivery!

Paradoxically, many training professionals passionately believe that their technical expertise and platform skills are the key reasons for effective transfer. Unfortunately, there is no evidence that well-delivered, entertaining training delivery has **in itself** any effect on transfer. What **does** have an effect is the way a good (and perhaps even brilliant and entertaining) trainer creates the conditions for learner sharing.

In a carefully constructed atmosphere of trust and camaraderie, participants are usually willing to share their best nuggets of effective practice. These are quickly snapped up by needy colleagues and immediately transferred. Necessity is also the mother of learning transfer!

STAGE 4: THE DELIVERY

TRAINER EFFECTIVENESS (1)

✓ Ensure that all trainers used by the organisation are qualified as facilitators as well as trainers

✓ Use trainers who understand and have a commitment to the goals of the training

✓ Check that trainers display genuine enthusiasm for the subject matter

STAGE 4: THE DELIVERY

TRAINER EFFECTIVENESS (2)

- ✓ Ensure that trainers are qualified as instructors

- ✓ Check that trainers understand learning design

- ✓ Ensure that trainers can use multiple communication media

ACTION TIPS

STAGE 4: THE DELIVERY

TRAINER EFFECTIVENESS (3)

☑ Ensure that trainers understand the industry

☑ Check that trainers know the organisation's strategy

☑ Ensure that trainers know where the training fits into that strategy

☑ Ensure trainers prepare meticulously for their programmes

☑ Check that trainers prepare 'Plan B' in readiness for multiple eventualities during the training

☑ Monitor that the training room is in full readiness mode before the first participant arrives

STAGE 4: THE DELIVERY
TRAINER'S UNDERSTANDING OF CONTEXT

In order to exploit this key factor (often neglected in transfer-low training events):

☑ Email participants before the course with specific, training context questions such as:
  - What are your key job objectives?
  - What are the main issues/ problems facing you at the moment?
  - Please give some specific examples of how you hope to use this training back on the job

☑ Wherever possible, arrange meetings with future participants to discuss the context of the training

☑ During the training event, refer to specific job issues as examples

☑ When conducting practical sessions, assign participants to learning activities according to their stated needs/ issues/ situation

STAGE 4: THE DELIVERY

TRAINING EVENT CLIMATE (1)

Never forget how important atmosphere, environment and ambience are to learning transfer.

Before the course:

☑ When welcoming participants, take the time to put them at ease by allowing mingling and exchange (even before the 'icebreaker'). This means insisting on a course venue that has adequate space for such important extra-curricular activities

☑ Use ambient music to relax participants and take away feelings of over-urgency and/ or school-like apprehension

☑ Create a convivial and non-threatening visual environment in the training room to enhance the atmosphere of friendliness and sharing

(One Australian participant at a course at the Master Trainer Institute in France remarked, on entering the training space, 'Gee, it looks like a flipping Romper Room in here!' – a statement we took as a compliment.)

ACTION TIPS

STAGE 4: THE DELIVERY
TRAINING EVENT CLIMATE (2)

During the course:

☑ Invite contributions from experienced participants and provide the time and space for questions and comments, rather than hogging all the limelight yourself

☑ Reward participants for sharing their experience and tips (verbally or otherwise) and emphasise the importance of sharing as an underlying theme or leitmotiv of the course

ACTION TIPS

STAGE 4: THE DELIVERY

Basically, the action tips in this section help training professionals answer the following question:

Do you fill the room with your brilliance and erudition or do you leave some space for learners to 'do it themselves' and meet their own learning needs?

ACTION TIPS

STAGE 5: THE RETURN TO WORK
KEY FACTORS

This is the critical stage. At least eight of the 17 factors have a strong influence on the return to work – the make or break moment when the newly trained skills and knowledge can be turned into performance improvement or left to wilt and die.

STAGE 1	STAGE 2	STAGE 3	STAGE 4	STAGE 5
The Need	Design & Development of Training	Initiation	The Delivery	The Return to Work

1. Organisational support for learning
2. Organisational linkage of training
3. Quality focus of the organisation
4. Learner's organisational level
5. Learner's job design
6. Learner's motivation to attend training
7. Clarity of learner's job
8. Learner's job autonomy
9. Perceived relevance of training
10. Training linked to learner's job purpose
11. Career utility of training
12. Trainer effectiveness
13. Trainer's understanding of context
14. Training event climate
15. Learning transfer management
16. Peer support for training
17. Opportunities to use the learning

STAGE 5: THE RETURN TO WORK

EXPLANATION

All the action tips suggested for this stage are prompted by the seemingly obvious (but almost always neglected) factors clustering together to tell us that learning will not yield results unless it is used back at work.

ACTION TIPS

STAGE 5: THE RETURN TO WORK

ORGANISATIONAL SUPPORT FOR LEARNING (1)

The level of support an organisation gives to training depends on how top management perceives the training function. There are many ways in which the people responsible for learning and development can build a reputation and influence the minds of the people on the top floor.

To use that distasteful but unforgettable analogy – a reputation is like a fart in the lift...it reaches every floor!

 Don't do it unless it's strategic!
Don't be tempted to do 'feel good' training because there's usually very little in the content of this type of training that can actually be used back on the job. Sometimes middle or even senior management will push you to do an off-the-shelf, motivational programme that they themselves have attended or heard about. Resist! Use ROI arguments. Question the take-away value and the performance improvement results of the training until they can really quantify the good which the 'feel good' factor will do to the organisation. Acting in this way will guarantee that training is seen as an important, results-bearing activity. Accordingly, organisational support for training will increase.

STAGE 5: THE RETURN TO WORK
ORGANISATIONAL SUPPORT FOR LEARNING (2)

 Don't do it unless it's strategic – exceptions to this rule:
Occasionally senior management feel very strongly about implementing training that has no obvious return to work value. They believe that the 'feel good' factor will make people proud to be part of the organisation. They hope it will reduce staff turnover and that it will help keep the organisation up there among the most attractive employers of the region/ country. Well…why not? Maybe that's enough vaguely stated return on investment to enable you to swallow your professional pride and do the training!

Seriously, we know of two top flight organisations that readily admit that a couple of their expensive management 'seminars' are really only PR exercises to maintain prestige and motivation. For more on this 'psychological capital' approach to measurement, see *Training Evaluation Pocketbook*, by Paul Donovan and John Townsend.

ACTION TIPS

STAGE 5: THE RETURN TO WORK
ORGANISATIONAL SUPPORT FOR LEARNING (3)

☑ Sit with business unit/ departmental managers as they develop their strategic plans, suggesting how training can support/ affect their results

☑ Never miss an opportunity to link training to a 'good news' story. As training professionals we are responsible for our own publicity and public relations strategy. Like this, the reputation of the training function grows and engenders more support – a virtuous circle. The opposite (the vicious circle) is obviously also true. A few lukewarm news stories about training can result in our becoming known simply as *'that nice man/ lady in training'*

☑ Never be heard to say *'I wish management would support training'* because you know that it's in **your** hands

ACTION TIPS

STAGE 5: THE RETURN TO WORK

QUALITY FOCUS OF THE ORGANISATION

✓ Build a relationship with the Quality Assurance Director (or similar portfolio). Work out how you can help each other to promote quality improvement within the firm

✓ Secure your membership on the Quality Council of your organisation. If there isn't one in existence, set one up. In this way you can demonstrate your commitment to quality in the organisation and in doing so, you'll make many friends for the training function

✓ Be a beacon of quality in everything you do. Develop a vision of quality for the training function. Become an oasis of quality in the organisational landscape so that senior managers use you as an example: *'I wish other units behaved like that.'*

STAGE 5: THE RETURN TO WORK
LEARNER'S ORGANISATIONAL LEVEL (1)
LEARNER'S JOB AUTONOMY (1)

One of the key findings from the research is that the higher a person's position in the organisational hierarchy, the more learning they transfer back to the workplace. This is obviously linked to job autonomy, in that the fewer the number of bosses you have breathing down your financial or behavioural neck, the more you are likely to get done on returning to work. We know intuitively that higher-echelon, more autonomous employees can achieve more – if they want to.

ACTION TIPS

STAGE 5: THE RETURN TO WORK
LEARNER'S ORGANISATIONAL LEVEL (2)
LEARNER'S JOB AUTONOMY (2)

There's not much the training function can do about organisational levels and autonomy in terms of creating action plans. Many innovative organisations have taken, however, an analogical approach to increasing employees' rank by encouraging autonomy. Some carefully choose the job titles of their staff while others allow people to take decisions independently in certain situations. For example:

- Nordstrom call all employees 'Associate'; CERN have 'Surface Technicians' but no 'Floor Sweepers'
- Asea Brown Boveri (ABB) introduced self-managing teams which made decisions ranging from simple housekeeping matters to complex issues such as new hires and compensation

Sit down with top management and review opportunities for allowing people this kind of freedom to put training messages into practice

ACTION TIPS

STAGE 5: THE RETURN TO WORK

CAREER UTILITY OF TRAINING (1)
LEARNING TRANSFER MANAGEMENT (1)

Include in all managers' job descriptions the requirement to conduct **post-course briefings** during which they:

☑ Confirm and agree on those specific performance goals outlined during the pre-course briefing, and demonstrate how their achievement might affect the learner's career opportunities

☑ Review the content and conduct of the training programme and agree on an evaluation to be recorded and shared with colleagues

☑ Agree on a time and place for the learner to share as much of their learning as possible with other members of their team

☑ Draw up a plan concerning opportunities to use the learning and the peer support needed while applying the learning (see details on following pages)

ACTION TIPS

STAGE 5: THE RETURN TO WORK

CAREER UTILITY OF TRAINING (2)
LEARNING TRANSFER MANAGEMENT (2)

In the weeks and months following a training event, the learner's manager should:

☑ Conduct regular meetings with the learner to review on-the-job applications of the learning and, by doing so, demonstrate that there is a structured approach to the implementation of new skills. Include these reviews in more formal sessions such as performance appraisals. Always look at career possibilities based on the progress that has been made in applying the learning

☑ Regularly measure/ evaluate the effectiveness of the training
(This may entail completing questionnaires provided by the training department, ie Level 3: Behaviour Evaluation. See also *Training Evaluation Pocketbook*, by Paul Donovan and John Townsend)

☑ Take an ongoing **informal** interest in the application of the trained skills and give regular feedback as to how well the learning is being applied
(The research has shown that the simple fact of a boss taking interest in the application of newly trained skills makes performance improvement almost a self-fulfilling prophesy)

ACTION TIPS

STAGE 5: THE RETURN TO WORK

PEER SUPPORT FOR TRAINING (1)

Following the identification and planning of tasks and/ or projects as mentioned on the previous page, the returning learner's manager should:

 Provide the learner with a skills and knowledge matrix of 'who can help' to show who to go to for help or coaching in the kind of skills being practised

Example:
A trainer in a large company returned from a train-the-trainer seminar needing to practise 'pinboarding' skills (using a large paper board to replace sleep-inducing slides for visual aids, facilitating discussions, etc). Her 'who can help' matrix pointed to a colleague who used the boards in his management seminars. He invited her to assist him during a session on problem-solving. She took charge of recording and sorting participant contributions on the boards, leaving him more freedom to concentrate on eliciting useful information from the group. A truly 'win-win' example of peer support which can surely be duplicated in many a coaching situation.

ACTION TIPS

STAGE 5: THE RETURN TO WORK

PEER SUPPORT FOR TRAINING (2)

Sometime during the days/ weeks following the return to work the learner's manager could:

 Organise some kind of 'brown bag' lunch sessions (ie outside 'normal' working hours) so that the learner can share key learning points from the training with those of their colleagues for whom they would be useful

 Create 'learning sets' – pairs of team members (or trios or more) who get together regularly to compare notes on how the application of new skills is progressing and/ or who work together on the tasks and projects the manager has set up for this purpose. These learning sets could be composed of buddies who attended the same course, or else a returning learner together with a designated coach/ mentor who will help smooth the way for the practice of the new skills

ACTION TIPS

STAGE 5: THE RETURN TO WORK

OPPORTUNITIES TO USE THE LEARNING

In the weeks and months following training, the learner's manager should:

☑ Create specific tasks and/ or projects where the learner can put the new skills and knowledge into practice

☑ Conduct a feasibility analysis with the learner as to how they can apply the learning

☑ Accept that the learner's productivity will dip as the practising of new skills slows down performance (before taking off to new levels!)

☑ Reward overtly the use of the learning and discourage slipping back to old behaviours

Example:
Before running a supervisory skills course, one of the authors met with the line managers of the supervisors attending, in order to agree on the projects which needed to be tackled when trainees returned to work. This enabled bosses to see and agree where they could support the trainees by giving them opportunities to use their new found skills back at work.

STAGE 5: THE RETURN TO WORK

SUMMARY

All the action tips you've just read could be summed up as follows:

If the organisation is serious about increasing learning transfer, then it must insist that returning learners' managers conduct **post-course briefings** to sustain the momentum achieved by the course and to plan comprehensively the application of learning to performance improvement.

THE LEARNING TRANSFER TEST

How 'transfer-friendly' is your
organisation?

THE LEARNING TRANSFER TEST

EXPLANATION

On the following pages you'll find our 50 item transfer test which will give you the opportunity of determining how well your own organisation is coping with the issue of learning transfer. Each item is a statement of best practice in the area of learning transfer, worded as if it applied to you.

For each item, you simply give a score of 0, 1 or 2 depending on the extent to which you agree that the statement applies to your organisation.

0 = Do not agree at all that this statement applies to my organisation
1 = Agree to some extent that this statement applies to my organisation
2 = Fully agree that this statement applies to my organisation

Having completed the test add up your score (page by page).

The highest possible score is 100 points or...100% transfer-friendly

How did you do?

Perhaps this will provide you with some 'ammunition' for your next meeting with senior management.

Good luck!

THE LEARNING TRANSFER TEST

LEARNING TRANSFER TEST

	SCORE 0-2
1. Our organisation believes in training and has included references to people development in its mission statement	
2. Our organisation has a rigorous system for identifying those training needs that are relevant to achieving its goals	
3. Training professionals never complain that management doesn't support training	
4. Our training function actively promotes itself as a serious organisational, problem-solving partner to management	
5. Training professionals regularly participate in business unit/departmental strategic planning meetings	
Total page score	

THE LEARNING TRANSFER TEST

LEARNING TRANSFER TEST

SCORE
0-2

6. Training professionals assist management in briefing employees on how training courses relate to organisational goals	
7. We try and avoid 'feel good' training unless senior management make a clear strategic case for it	
8. Training professionals regularly ask the three key 'training need' questions to senior management: (i) What are you trying to achieve/avoid? (ii) What must people in the organisation do to help you get there? (iii) What must they learn in order to provide this help?	
9. Our organisation seeks to give job holders as much autonomy as possible to help them achieve their objectives	
10. The training department has obtained meaningful accreditation for learners attending courses	

Total page score

THE LEARNING TRANSFER TEST

LEARNING TRANSFER TEST

SCORE
0-2

11. All the training courses our employees attend (in-company and public) are linked to their job purpose	
12. The titles and content of all the courses we send people on reflect specific job issues	
13. All the exercises and activities in our in-company courses simulate the job situation of the majority of participants	
14. All our course designs contain opportunities for learners to plan how to apply the learning to specific job situations	
15. All our courses contain exercises which allow for existing 'best practice' sharing	
Total page score	

THE LEARNING TRANSFER TEST

LEARNING TRANSFER TEST

SCORE
0-2

16. All our courses contain 'case conferences' where participants provide their own problems/issues for group solution-seeking		
17. All the handouts and tools which are given out on training courses are transferable and usable for all participants		
18. Our course venues provide adequate space for participants to associate and exchange		
19. Our course designs allow for a participant 'get-together' (even before an icebreaker in the training room)		
20. We prepare ambient music to be played at all our in-company courses to help participants to relax		

Total page score

THE LEARNING TRANSFER TEST

LEARNING TRANSFER TEST

SCORE
0-2

21. Our training rooms are designed to be visually non-threatening. They look friendly and welcoming	☐
22. We design 15 minute stretch and coffee/tea breaks into our courses at least every 90 minutes	☐
23. Our managers communicate clear expectations of forthcoming training to future learners	☐
24. Learners' managers explain to them the advantages of forthcoming training according to the learner's motivational profile	☐
25. Learners' managers clarify their job descriptions with them before sending them on training	☐

Total page score ☐

THE LEARNING TRANSFER TEST

LEARNING TRANSFER TEST

SCORE
0-2

26. Learners' managers clarify the degree of authority and freedom they will be allowed in applying new skills after training ☐

27. Learners' managers coach participants in anticipation of training ☐

28. Learners' managers arrange pre-course briefings and agree on specific goals to be met as a result of training ☐

29. Managers contract with learners' team members prior to training as to how the learner's job will be covered during the course ☐

30. Wherever possible, learners' managers send pairs of 'learning buddies' to the same course ☐

Total page score ☐

THE LEARNING TRANSFER TEST

LEARNING TRANSFER TEST

SCORE
0-2

31. Our trainers email participants before courses with specific training context and content questions ☐

32. Our trainers meet with future participants to discuss the context of training ☐

33. Our trainers understand the industry in which they work ☐

34. Our trainers understand the strategy of the organisation ☐

35. Our trainers know the purpose of the training and where it fits into the organisation's overall strategy ☐

Total page score ☐

THE LEARNING TRANSFER TEST

LEARNING TRANSFER TEST

	SCORE 0-2
36. Our trainers understand and speak the workplace jargon of the trainees	
37. Our trainers' background and experience provide credibility to our programmes	
38. Our trainers always behave as role models for the learning objectives of the programme (walk the talk)	
39. During in-company training courses our trainers refer to specific job issues as examples	
40. During in-company training courses our trainers assign participants to activities according to their stated needs	
Total page score	

THE LEARNING TRANSFER TEST

LEARNING TRANSFER TEST

SCORE
0-2

41. During in-company training courses, our trainers invite contributions from experienced participants and provide time for questions and comments from the others	
42. During in-company training courses, our trainers reward (verbally or otherwise) participants who share ideas and solutions	
43. All our trainers have been trained in facilitation skills as well as 'classic' platform skills	
44. Following training, managers draw up a 'who can help' matrix to show who can help returning learners to use new skills	
45. Managers organise 'brown bag lunch' sessions where returning learners share training messages with colleagues	
Total page score	

THE LEARNING TRANSFER TEST

LEARNING TRANSFER TEST

SCORE
0-2

46. Learners' managers create specific tasks and/ or projects for learners to put new skills into practice	☐
47. Managers create 'learning sets' of duos or trios of 'buddies' who will work with learners to smooth the way for the practice of new skills	☐
48. Learners' managers accept that productivity will dip for a period while learners practise new skills	☐
49. Learners' managers overtly encourage/reward the use of new learning	☐
50. Managers regularly discuss with learners how training will help their career	☐
Total test score (% Transfer-friendliness score of organisation)	☐

FURTHER INFORMATION

REFERENCES

For any reader who would like to examine our thinking further, the publications listed below were those we used to provide specific support when writing the book.

Baldwin T. T & Ford J.K, *Transfer of Training: A Review and Directions for Future Research*, Personnel Psychology, 41, 63-105 (1988)

Barrett A & O'Connell P, *Does Training Generally Work? The Returns to In-Company Training*, Industrial and Labor Relations review, 54 (3) (2001)

Broad M.L & Newstrom J.W, *Transfer of Training*, Addison-Wesley

Cromwell S.E & Kolb J.A, *An Examination of Work Environment Support Factors Affecting Transfer of Supervisory Skills Training to the Workplace*, Human Resource Development Quarterly, 15 (4) (2004)

Facteau J, Dobbins G, Russell J, Ladd R & Kudisch J, *The influence of general perceptions of the training environment on penetrating motivation and perceived training transfer*, Journal of Management, 21, 1-25 (1995)

Goldstein I.L, *Training in organisation: Needs assessment, development and evaluation*, Monterey CA: Brooks/Cole (1986)

Kaufman R, *Resolving the (often deserved) attacks on training*, Performance Management 41 (6) (2002)

Kirkpatrick D.L, *Evaluating Training Programs, San Francisco*: Berrett-Koehler (1994)

Wexley K.N & Latham G.P, *Developing and Training Human Resources in Organisations*, Journal of European Industrial Training, 31 (4), 283-296 (2007)

FURTHER INFORMATION

RECOMMENDED READING

Anderson V, *Research Methods in Human Resource Management*, London:CIPD (2009)

Bee F & Bee R, *Learning Needs Analysis and Evaluation*, London: Institute of Personnel and Development (1997)

Boselie P, *Strategic Human Resource Management*, Maidenhead Berkshire: McGraw-Hill (2010)

Cascio W.F, *Costing Human Resources*, Mason OH: South-Western Publishing (1999)

Donovan P & Townsend J, *Training Evaluation Pocketbook*, Management Pocketbooks (2004)

Donovan P & Townsend J, *Training Needs Analysis Pocketbook*, Management Pocketbooks (2004)

Easterby-Smith M, *Evaluating Management Development, Training & Education*, Gower Publishing Ltd (1994)

Hamblin A.C, *Evaluation and Control of Training*, McGraw-Hill New York (1974)

McGuire D & Molbjerg Jorgensen K, *Human Resource Development*, Sage (2011)

Sugrue B, *State of the Industry. ASTD's annual review of US and international trends in workplace learning and performance*, ASTD (2003)

About the Authors

Dr Paul Donovan
Paul is School Director of Teaching and Learning at the School of Business, National University of Ireland Maynooth. He has extensive management experience and has conducted a wide range of HRD assignments in Western Europe and Asia.

Paul's professional interests include researching evaluation of training and development interventions where he has identified easy-to-use surrogate measures as effective replacements for time-consuming and expensive evaluation initiatives. He has edited seven books in a series of management texts.

Contact
To contact Paul, email paul.donovan@nuim.ie or phone 00 353 1 7086627

John Townsend, BA MA MCIPD
John has built a reputation internationally as a leading trainer of trainers. He is the founder of the highly-regarded Master Trainer Institute, a total learning facility located just outside Geneva which draws trainers and facilitators from around the world. He set up the Institute after 30 years' experience in international consulting and human resource management positions in the UK, France, the United States and Switzerland – notably as European Director of Executive Development with GTE in Geneva where he had training responsibility for over 800 managers in 15 countries. John has published a number of management and professional guides and regularly contributes articles to leading management and training journals.

Other titles in the Pocketbook series by the same authors